AGES 5-7

SPELLING
WORKBOOK
FOR KIDS

Lesson 1

THE, OF, AND, AT, THAT, CAT, MAT, SAT, HAT, RAT

Read the spelling words below and then write the words in the spaces provided.

and
at
cat
hat
mat
of
rat
sat
that
the

Complete the sentences using your spelling words.

I have a pet _____.

When it is cold I wear a _____.

Me _____ my friend like to play.

_____ is a big house.

I _____ in the chair.

Find and circle the spelling words in the puzzle.

AND	R B C D S U Z
AT	H A N A P J E
CAT	A A T A T T H
HAT	T O A G T H B
MAT	
OF	N R F A E E J
RAT	H T S T H A T
SAT	A M A T P W D
THAT	
THE	

Learn and Practice
Over 350 Essential Words

Get Ready to Spell!

Hi! Are you ready to have fun and learn too? This book contains **36 weeks** of spelling lessons that are designed to help master the essential words for **first grade and beyond**.

Each lesson contains **10 spelling words** with four pages of activities. Each activity helps to reinforce learning and memory of the spelling words. These activities include tracing, fill in the blanks, complete the sentences, find the words, recognizing rhymes, and more!

For each lesson remember to:

* Read the word and practice saying it out loud

* Trace the word to increase muscle memory

* Do the activities

* **Have fun!**

Lesson 1

THE, OF, AND, AT,
THAT, CAT, MAT, SAT,
HAT, RAT

Read the spelling words below and then write the words in the spaces provided.

and

at

cat

hat

mat

of

rat

sat

that

the

Complete the sentences using your spelling words.

I have a pet _____.

When it is cold I wear a _____.

Me _____ my friend like to play.

_____ is a big house.

I _____ in the chair.

Find and circle the spelling words in the puzzle.

AND
AT
CAT
HAT
MAT
OF
RAT
SAT
THAT
THE

R	B	C	D	S	U	Z
H	A	N	A	P	J	E
A	A	T	A	T	T	H
T	O	A	G	T	H	B
N	R	F	A	E	E	J
H	T	S	T	H	A	T
A	M	A	T	P	W	D

1 Circle the correct spelling for each word.

1	amd	and	anb
2	at	et	ta
3	kat	cet	cat
4	hta	hat	jat
5	mat	maat	mot
6	ov	of	fo
7	ratt	rath	rat
8	sta	sat	sot
9	that	thet	tath
10	tha	teh	the

Fill in the missing letter in the spelling words below.

a __ d   ha __

c __ t   a __

t __ e   sa __

r __ t   ma __

__ f   tha __

Circle the words that rhyme in each row.

hat   sat   sit   rat

that   the   mat   at

and   sand   cat   land

bat   but   fat   bad

Lesson 2

TO, IN, IS, YOU, MAN, CAN, RAN, TAN, ANY, PUT

Read the spelling words below and then write the words in the spaces provided.

to

in

is

you

man

can

ran

tan

any

put

Complete the sentences using your spelling words.

I _____ away.

The sun made me _____.

The pizza is _____ the oven.

_____ that down.

I went _____ school.

Find and circle the spelling words in the puzzle.

ANY
CAN
IN
IS
MAN
PUT
RAN
TAN
TO
YOU

T	A	N	I	I	U
A	R	C	A	N	N
N	A	S	U	G	I
Y	N	O	P	N	J
T	Y	O	A	U	S
E	O	M	B	I	T

2 Circle the correct spelling for each word.

1	to	tou	tu
2	un	in	en
3	ya	yu	you
4	is	iz	iss
5	mann	maat	man
6	cam	can	con
7	arn	ram	ran
8	tam	tan	tab
9	ani	ony	any
10	put	putt	puut

Fill in the missing letter in the spelling words below.

t __ __

y __ u

m __ n

r __ n

__ ny

i __ __

__ s

ca __

ta __

tha __

Circle the words that rhyme in each row.

man	sat	sit	can
that	the	man	ran
pet	sand	cat	met
you	tan	boo	bad

Lesson 3

WITH, NEAR, THEY, ALL, AM, OUT, SIT, HIT, FIT, BIT

Read the spelling words below and then write the words in the spaces provided.

with

near

they

all

am

out

sit

hit

fit

bit

Complete the sentences using your spelling words.

_____ down in the chair.

I _____ happy.

_____ are all here.

I brought my lunch _____ me.

I _____ the punching bag.

Find and circle the spelling words in the puzzle.

ALL
AM
BIT
FIT
HIT
NEAR
OUT
SIT
THEY
WITH

A	T	T	V	R	Y	E
T	I	H	A	B	I	T
H	P	E	E	S	I	T
O	N	A	W	Y	W	V
U	H	L	I	F	J	J
T	R	L	T	P	I	M
N	C	M	H	U	A	T

3 Circle the correct spelling for each word.

1	wit	witt	with
2	near	neer	neare
3	the	they	thee
4	all	oll	al
5	an	amm	am
6	out	ot	uot
7	sat	sitt	sit
8	hit	hitt	hiit
9	fitt	fit	fat
10	bite	bitt	bit

Fill in the missing letter in the spelling words below.

wi __ h   ne _ r

th __ y   a __ l

a __   ou __

s __ t   __ it

__ it   bi __

Circle the words that rhyme in each row.

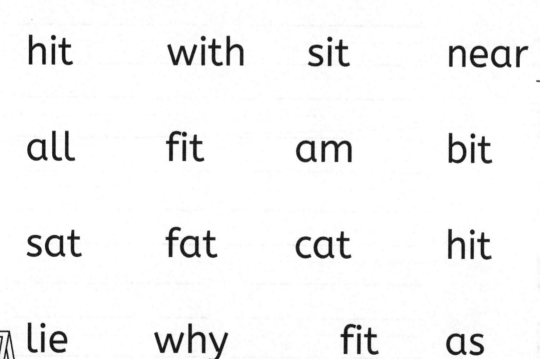

hit   with   sit   near _____

all   fit   am   bit

sat   fat   cat   hit

lie   why   fit   as

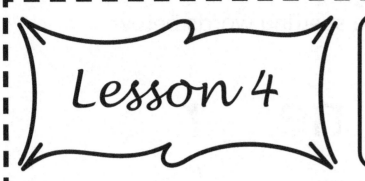

Lesson 4

AT, BE, CAME, DO, GET, EAT, BIG, PIG, DIG, FIG

Read the spelling words below and then write the words in the spaces provided.

at

be

came

do

get

eat

big

pig

dig

fig

Complete the sentences using your spelling words.

The _____ lives at the farm.

_____ your homework.

Time to _____ dinner.

_____ the hole.

_____ in the car.

Find and circle the spelling words in the puzzle.

AT
BE
BIG
CAME
DIG
DO
EAT
FIG
GET
PIG

B	C	D	I	G	Q
I	A	A	B	E	F
G	T	G	M	T	I
M	I	Z	A	E	G
P	D	E	T	D	F
F	G	E	T	G	O

4 Circle the correct spelling for each word.

1 bee   be   bii

2 come   came   cam

3 doo   do   doy

4 gut   get   got

5 eat   ate   eet

6 bug   byg   big

7 pug   pigg   pig

8 dug   dig   deg

9 at   et   aht

10 figg   phig   fig

Fill in the missing letter in the spelling words below.

b ___ ___   ca ___ e

d ___ ___   ge ___ ___

e ___ t   bi ___ ___

p ___ g   di ___ ___

a ___ ___   f ___ g

Circle the words that rhyme in each row.

be	big	can	pig
dig	do	fig	has
do	why	you	bet
but	get	yes	let

Lesson 5

ATE, BROWN, BUT, HAVE, HE, INTO, MAP, CAP, NAP, LAP

Read the spelling words below and then write the words in the spaces provided.

ate

brown

but

have

he

into

map

cap

nap

lap

Complete the sentences using your spelling words.

I _____ breakfast.

I was tired so I took a _____.

My shirt is _____.

If you are lost look at the _____

The cat sat on my _____.

Find and circle the spelling words in the puzzle.

ATE
BROWN
BUT
CAP
HAVE
HE
INTO
LAP
MAP
NAP

N	A	P	M	B	L	U
X	L	A	P	R	A	U
I	C	H	P	O	T	W
M	N	A	E	W	E	E
A	F	T	P	N	V	T
P	P	E	O	A	U	X
L	Z	G	H	B	F	Y

5 Circle the correct spelling for each word.

1 ait   ayt   ate

2 brn   brown   brone

3 butt   but   bot

4 have   hav   hove

5 hee   hey   he

6 into   intoo   intyu

7 mapp   mop   map

8 capp   cap   cop

9 nap   nup   knap

10 lapp   lop   lap

Fill in the missing letter in the spelling words below.

a __ e   br __ wn

b __ t   h __ ve

__ e   in __

m __ p   ca __

n __ p   la __

Circle the words that rhyme in each row.

eat	map	cop	cap
lap	can	nap	no
into	mop	his	top
ate	but	bot	late

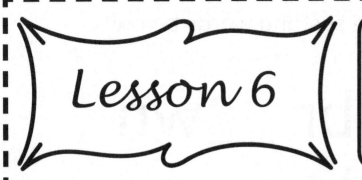

Lesson 6

ARE, DID, RAN, SHE, SOON, TOO, BACK, SACK, TACK, BLACK

Read the spelling words below and then write the words in the spaces provided.

are

did

ran

she

soon

too

back

sack

tack

black

Complete the sentences using your spelling words.

_____ is my friend.

I will be _____ soon.

I _____ away.

It is going to rain _____.

I ate _____ much food.

Find and circle the spelling words in the puzzle.

ARE
BACK
BLACK
DID
RAN
SACK
SHE
SOON
TACK
TOO

T	Q	H	M	R	A	N
S	A	I	D	I	D	K
G	W	C	H	T	C	E
C	B	E	K	A	R	S
P	H	A	L	A	T	A
S	Y	B	C	W	O	C
S	O	O	N	K	O	K

Circle the correct spelling for each word.

1	ar	are	har
2	dud	didd	did
3	ran	rann	rhan
4	she	sha	se
5	soone	sune	soon
6	too	tu	tuu
7	bak	bac	back
8	sak	sack	sac
9	tack	tac	takk
10	blak	blac	black

Fill in the missing letter in the spelling words below.

a __ e   di __

r __ n   sh __

s __ on   to __

ba __ k   sac __

t __ ck   bla __ k

Circle the words that rhyme in each row.

back   why   black   rat

hello   sack   to   tack

ran   what   man   tree

soon   drive   cup   moon

Lesson 7

NOW, ON, OUR, SAW, SAY, WANT, HOT, NOT, LOT, POT

Read the spelling words below and then write the words in the spaces provided.

now

on

our

saw

say

want

hot

not

lot

pot

Complete the sentences using your spelling words.

The pillow is _____ the bed.

When it is _____ I wear shorts.

I cooked food in the _____.

_____ dog is named Max.

We are leaving right _____ .

Find and circle the spelling words in the puzzle.

HOT
LOT
NOT
NOW
ON
OUR
POT
SAW
SAY
WANT

M	A	W	H	L	P
O	O	H	T	O	O
N	U	N	O	T	T
S	A	R	Y	T	D
W	A	S	A	W	S
O	N	Y	N	O	T

1   nwa   naw   now

2   on   en   onn

3   our   oru   ower

4   swa   saw   sah

5   sah   say   saye

6   want   wantt   wont

7   hott   hhot   hot

8   not   nott   nout

9   lott   lot   lok

10   pot   pott   phot

Fill in the missing letter in the spelling words below.

n__w   o__

o__r   sa__

s__y   wan__

h__t   no__

l__t   po__

Circle the words that rhyme in each row.

hot   yes   not   saw

say   want   hey   knot

glass   pot   bird   lot

 now   grass   car   cow

Lesson 8

RIDE, SO, THERE, THEY, WAS, WELL, SICK, KICK, LICK, BRICK

Read the spelling words below and then write the words in the spaces provided.

ride

so

there

they

was

well

sick

kick

lick

brick

Complete the sentences using your spelling words.

I went to _____ on the horse.

The house is made out of _____

I stayed home because I am _____ .

You _____ with you're tongue.

I like to _____ the ball.

Find and circle the spelling words in the puzzle.

BRICK
KICK
LICK
RIDE
SICK
SO
THERE
THEY
WAS
WELL

T	H	E	R	E	A	M
V	K	O	Y	Y	W	L
R	S	B	E	T	E	I
K	I	H	R	X	L	C
I	T	D	W	I	L	K
C	Q	U	E	A	C	I
K	S	I	C	K	S	K

8 Circle the correct spelling for each word.

1	ride	rhide	ridy
2	soo	sho	so
3	thier	there	ther
4	they	thee	thyy
5	wass	was	wazz
6	wel	wehl	well
7	sick	sik	sicc
8	kik	kic	kick
9	lik	lick	licc
10	brick	bric	bricc

Fill in the missing letter in the spelling words below.

r__de   s__

th__re   th__y

w__s   wel__

si__k   kic__

li__k   bri__k

Circle the words that rhyme in each row.

lick	write	sick	us
brick	sure	for	kick
guy	they	hot	hey
ride	hide	buy	boy

Lesson 9

WENT, WHAT, YES, THIS, WHO, WILL, TOP, MOP, HOP, DROP

Read the spelling words below and then write the words in the spaces provided.

went

what

yes

this

who

will

top

mop

hop

drop

Complete the sentences using your spelling words.

I _____ to the beach.

Time to _____ the dirty floor.

The frog likes to _____.

_____ time is it?

I climbed to the _____ .

Find and circle the spelling words in the puzzle.

DROP
HOP
MOP
THIS
TOP
WENT
WHAT
WHO
WILL
YES

R	J	W	H	A	T	Y
W	A	Z	M	O	P	W
E	D	R	O	P	L	H
N	M	P	T	L	Z	O
T	O	S	I	H	P	D
H	E	W	J	O	I	E
Y	P	W	T	Y	C	S

1	wen	wennt	went
2	what	wat	watt
3	yess	yas	yes
4	thiss	this	thiz
5	whoo	who	hoo
6	will	wil	wall
7	topp	top	tup
8	mop	mopp	mup
9	hopp	hop	hhop
10	drop	dropp	drap

Fill in the missing letter in the spelling words below.

w __ nt   wha __

y __ s   thi __

w __ o   wi __ l

to __   mo __

__ op   dr __ p

Circle the words that rhyme in each row.

end   drop   mop   turn

down   hop   top   out

went   box   does   lent

hole   work   mole   all

Lesson 10

PLEASE, PRETTY, WITH, UNDER, WHITE, SOCK, ROCK, LOCK, DOCK, CLOCK

Read the spelling words below and then write the words in the spaces provided.

please

pretty

under

white

with

sock

rock

lock

dock

clock

Complete the sentences using your spelling words.

The boat is tied to the _____.

_____ the door.

The _____ is on the ground.

I put the _____ on my foot.

_____ help me.

Find and circle the spelling words in the puzzle.

CLOCK
DOCK
LOCK
PLEASE
PRETTY
ROCK
SOCK
UNDER
WHITE
WITH

C	L	O	C	K	K	D	Y
P	L	E	A	S	E	T	W
J	K	R	K	K	T	C	T
I	W	C	O	E	J	U	A
H	O	H	R	C	X	N	W
S	H	P	I	E	K	D	I
L	O	C	K	T	Q	E	T
D	O	C	K	S	E	R	H

10 Circle the correct spelling for each word.

1	plese	pleas	please
2	prety	pretty	prety
3	unda	undr	under
4	white	whit	wite
5	witt	with	whyt
6	sock	sok	socc
7	rokk	rocc	rock
8	lock	locke	lok
9	dok	dack	dock
10	clock	clok	clocc

Fill in the missing letter in the spelling words below.

ple __ se   pret __ y

un __ er   wh __ te

w __ th   so __ k

r __ ck   lo __ k

d __ ck   cl __ ck

Circle the words that rhyme in each row.

clock	book	dock	mat
rock	other	lock	more
nut	mut	cop	mind
live	look	much	book

Lesson 11

AFTER. AGAIN, LET, MAY, OLD, STOP, JOB, ROB, MOB, SOB

Read the spelling words below and then write the words in the spaces provided.

after

again

let

may

old

stop

job

rob

mob

sob

Complete the sentences using your spelling words.

I'm going home _____ school.

My mom has a good _____.

_____ me inside please.

_____ driving so fast.

My grandfather is _____ .

Find and circle the spelling words in the puzzle.

AFTER
AGAIN
JOB
LET
MAY
MOB
OLD
ROB
SOB
STOP

A	F	T	E	R	C	J
O	X	T	K	N	B	O
S	E	E	I	O	S	B
L	O	A	M	O	T	A
R	G	B	U	L	O	O
A	O	V	C	D	P	V
O	G	B	M	A	Y	D

11 Circle the correct spelling for each word.

1   after   aftr   ater

2   agan   agian   again

3   lel   lett   let

4   mai   may   mayy

5   olde   ald   old

6   stop   stap   sopt

7   job   gob   jobe

8   robb   rob   rab

9   mobb   mab   mob

10   sob   sab   sobb

Fill in the missing letter in the spelling words below.

aft __ r   ag __ in

l __ t   ma __

o __ d   sto __

j __ b   ro __

m __ b   so __

Circle the words that rhyme in each row.

be   mob   sob   see

job   bad   rob   juice

let   chief   stun   met

this   may   find   lay

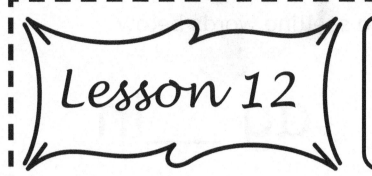

ASK, EVERY, FLY, GIVE, LIVE, READ, BUG, RUG, HUG, MUG

Read the spelling words below and then write the words in the spaces provided.

ask

every

fly

give

live

read

bug

rug

hug

mug

Complete the sentences using your spelling words.

_____ me a question.

I love to _____ books.

The _____ crawled outside.

A bird can _____ .

I poured coffee in the _____ .

Find and circle the spelling words in the puzzle.

ASK
BUG
EVERY
FLY
GIVE
HUG
LIVE
MUG
READ
RUG

C	Q	E	Z	Q	G	H
R	U	G	V	U	T	F
B	J	M	H	E	D	L
U	G	T	U	A	R	Y
G	I	O	E	G	U	Y
R	V	R	P	A	S	K
Q	E	L	I	V	E	G

Circle the correct spelling for each word.

1	ask	aks	asc
2	evry	every	everi
3	fly	fli	flyy
4	giav	giv	give
5	liv	lyv	live
6	red	read	raed
7	bug	bag	bugg
8	rugg	rag	rug
9	hag	hug	hugg
10	mugg	mag	mug

Fill in the missing letter in the spelling words below.

a __ k   eve __ y

f __ y   g __ ve

li __ e   rea __

b __ g   r __ g

h __ g   __ ug

Circle the words that rhyme in each row.

rug   roll   mug   tape

hug   bug   it   five

fly   out   time   bye

lead   go   read   try

Lesson 13

GOING, JUST, KNOW, IT, HE, WAS, CUT, NUT, SHUT, BUT

Read the spelling words below and then write the words in the spaces provided.

going

just

know

it

he

was

cut

nut

shut

but

Complete the sentences using your spelling words.

I _____ the bread with a knife.

_____ the door.

_____ is my friend.

I _____ how to read.

The movie _____ great.

Find and circle the spelling words in the puzzle.

BUT
CUT
GOING
HE
IT
JUST
KNOW
NUT
SHUT
WAS

B	U	T	T	Z	A	S
G	O	I	N	G	H	T
S	A	C	I	N	U	E
W	C	K	S	C	U	T
W	I	N	I	H	S	T
A	T	O	W	U	U	T
S	O	W	J	F	H	T

1 goin   going   giong

2 jus   juts   just

3 know   no   kno

4 ti   itt   it

5 he   ha   hee

6 was   waz   wos

7 cutt   cut   cute

8 nutt   nat   nut

9 shutt   shat   shut

10 butt   but   bat

Fill in the missing letter in the spelling words below.

go __ng   jus __

kn __ w   i __

__ e   wa __

c __ t   nu __

sh __ t   bu __

Circle the words that rhyme in each row.

be   but   got   shut

cut   team   nut   rid

he   she   for   me

no   plus   know   play

Lesson 14

ONCE, OPEN, ROUND, FOR, ONE, ARE, PET, LET, MET, WET

Read the spelling words below and then write the words in the spaces provided.

once

open

round

for

one

are

pet

let

met

wet

Complete the sentences using your spelling words.

_____ the door.

I want a _____ dog.

The rain is making me _____ .

We just _____ .

The ball is _____ .

Find and circle the spelling words in the puzzle.

ARE
FOR
LET
MET
ONCE
ONE
OPEN
PET
ROUND
WET

O	A	R	E	R	F	M
G	N	N	T	O	O	E
L	S	C	N	U	X	T
G	E	E	E	N	Z	A
B	P	T	R	D	E	F
O	P	E	T	N	X	O
W	E	T	O	J	O	R

1	one	onc	once
2	opan	apen	open
3	round	roand	rand
4	fore	for	four
5	on	one	uno
6	are	rar	ar
7	pet	pat	pit
8	lat	lut	let
9	mat	mut	met
10	wet	wat	wett

Fill in the missing letter in the spelling words below.

onc___   op ___n

ro ___ nd   fo ___ ___

o ___ e   ar ___ ___

p ___ ___ t   le ___ ___

m ___ ___ t   w ___ t

Circle the words that rhyme in each row.

wet   away   make   met

make   let   pet   week

away   true   one   done

side   kick   ride   off

Lesson 15

TAKE, THANK, THINK, WALK, AS, FROM, RED, BED, FED, WED

Read the spelling words below and then write the words in the spaces provided.

take

thank

think

walk

as

from

red

bed

fed

wed

Complete the sentences using your spelling words.

My favorite color is _____.

Make your _____.

I like to _____ the dog.

_____ you for the gift.

He leaped _____ his horse.

Find and circle the spelling words in the puzzle.

AS
BED
FED
FROM
RED
TAKE
THANK
THINK
WALK
WED

W	W	E	F	K	T	B
A	E	T	N	R	Q	E
L	D	A	H	D	O	D
K	H	I	E	I	P	M
T	S	R	D	B	N	K
A	T	A	K	E	L	K
O	F	I	F	E	D	P

Circle the correct spelling for each word.

1 take   tak   toke

2 tank   thank   thonk

3 thinc   think   tink

4 walk   wolk   wok

5 sa   az   as

6 fromm   fron   from

7 red   rad   read

8 bad   bed   bud

9 fed   fad   phed

10 wad   wed   wedd

Fill in the missing letter in the spelling words below.

t __ ke   th __ nk

th __ nk   w __ lk

a __   fro __

r __ ad   be __

f __ d   we __

Circle the words that rhyme in each row.

work   on   fed   wed

red   pull   lead   good

walk   take   lock   talk

this   miss   home   best

Lesson 16

OR, HAD, BY, WORD, WHAT, ALL, MEN, PEN, TEN, DEN

Read the spelling words below and then write the words in the spaces provided.

or

had

by

word

what

all

men

pen

ten

den

Complete the sentences using your spelling words.

The pig is in the _____.

_____ time is it?

Bears spend winter in their _____ .

I am _____ years old.

Let's _____ go outside.

Find and circle the spelling words in the puzzle.

| ALL |
| BY |
| DEN |
| HAD |
| MEN |
| OR |
| PEN |
| TEN |
| WHAT |
| WORD |

R W H A T D
D E N M R P
D G T O E C
P A W E D N
E L O A N Y
N L H R B O

1	orr	ar	or
2	had	hadd	hod
3	by	byy	bye
4	wod	ward	word
5	wat	what	whit
6	all	oll	al
7	man	menn	men
8	pen	pan	penn
9	tan	ten	tenn
10	dan	denn	den

Fill in the missing letter in the spelling words below.

o __ __

b __ __

wh __ t

m __ n

t __ n

ha __ __

wor __ __

a __ l

pe __ __

de __ __

Circle the words that rhyme in each row.

den   ten   talk   fair

some   mat   at   lat

pen   sell   men   hot

any   many   so   dog

Lesson 17

WERE, WE, WHEN, YOUR, CAN, SAID, USE, BAD, GLAD, MAD, SAD

Read the spelling words below and then write the words in the spaces provided.

were

we

when

your

can

said

use

bad

glad

mad

Complete the sentences using your spelling words.

I am _____ it's sunny out.

I am _____ I failed the test.

I am _____ I stubbed my toe.

_____ are going to play outside.

We _____ all there.

Find and circle the spelling words in the puzzle.

BAD
CAN
GLAD
MAD
SAID
USE
WE
WERE
WHEN
YOUR

T	J	N	W	C	Y	M
U	A	W	D	E	O	A
C	S	I	E	K	U	D
V	A	E	W	R	R	E
S	W	H	E	N	E	S
U	C	A	G	L	A	D
A	B	A	D	N	Q	Z

1	wer	were	where
2	we	wee	whe
3	wen	when	whan
4	your	you	yor
5	can	con	cann
6	sad	siad	said
7	us	yuse	use
8	bad	bod	badd
9	gladd	glad	glod
10	madd	mad	mod

Fill in the missing letter in the spelling words below.

we __ e   w __

wh __ n   you __

c __ n   sa __

u __ e   ba __

gl __ d   __ ad

Circle the words that rhyme in each row.

okay   glad   how   mad

mad   our   sad   issue

can   ran   only   bank

print   yeah   lake   make

Lesson 18

HOW, AN, EACH, WHICH, THEIR, DO, WIN, TIN, KID, LID

Read the spelling words below and then write the words in the spaces provided.

how

an

each

which

their

do

win

tin

kid

lid

Complete the sentences using your spelling words.

I hope we _____ the game.

The can is made of _____.

We know _____ other.

_____ did you do that?

The _____ is asleep.

Find and circle the spelling words in the puzzle.

AN
DO
EACH
HOW
KID
LID
THEIR
TIN
WHICH
WIN

H	F	W	H	I	C	H
O	E	W	P	X	T	D
W	P	A	Z	E	I	T
J	P	N	C	K	J	H
Z	I	T	O	H	Q	E
W	I	D	I	A	N	I
J	L	I	D	N	F	R

18 Circle the correct spelling for each word.

1 how   howe   haw

2 on   an   ann

3 eac   yach   each

4 wich   witch   which

5 theer   theyr   their

6 do   doo   du

7 winn   win   wan

8 tinn   tin   tyn

9 kid   kidd   kad

10 lidd   lad   lid

Fill in the missing letter in the spelling words below.

h __ w   a __ __

ea __ h   wh __ ch

th __ ir   d __ __

w __ n   ti __ __

k __ d   __ id

Circle the words that rhyme in each row.

stink   lid   kid   love

tin   go   one   win

witch   walk   come   rich

big   first   fig   gone

Lesson 19

IF, MANY, UP, OTHER, ABOUT, THEN, DOG, FOX, MOM, DAD

Read the spelling words below and then write the words in the spaces provided.

if

many

up

other

about

then

dog

fox

mom

dad

Complete the sentences using your spelling words.

I have a pet _____.

We were there the _____ day.

My _____ makes me lunch.

The plane is _____ in the air.

The _____ is red and has a tail.

Find and circle the spelling words in the puzzle.

ABOUT
DAD
DOG
FOX
IF
MANY
MOM
OTHER
THEN
UP

I	U	D	A	D	X	O
M	A	N	Y	O	T	N
H	A	O	F	M	E	D
D	B	Q	T	H	A	O
U	O	U	T	H	I	G
P	U	M	O	M	E	F
F	T	M	S	P	G	R

19

Circle the correct spelling for each word.

1	iff	if	yf
2	many	mony	manny
3	upp	up	ap
4	oter	other	otter
5	abot	abuott	about
6	than	thin	then
7	dogg	dog	dag
8	fox	fax	phox
9	mam	mom	mome
10	dad	did	dahd

Fill in the missing letter in the spelling words below.

i __

u __

abo __ t

d __ g

mo __

ma __ y

ot__er

th __

fo __

da __

Circle the words that rhyme in each row.

dog	wife	frog	sleep
up	term	yup	ten
clap	poor	vote	map
very	has	call	merry

Lesson 20

Read the spelling words below and then write the words in the spaces provided.

them

these

make

some

her

would

tell

fell

sell

bell

Complete the sentences using your spelling words.

_____ me a story.

I _____ down the stairs.

Ring the _____ .

I'm going to _____ a sandwich.

_____ but not all people were there.

Find and circle the spelling words in the puzzle.

BELL
FELL
HER
MAKE
SELL
SOME
TELL
THEM
THESE
WOULD

W	F	M	S	E	L	L
O	E	I	A	E	J	L
U	L	T	M	K	L	G
L	L	O	H	E	E	M
D	S	E	B	E	E	U
T	E	L	L	H	S	F
H	E	R	T	W	D	E

20

Circle the correct spelling for each word.

1	tham	them	themm
2	these	tese	thes
3	make	moke	mayk
4	som	sam	some
5	herr	he	her
6	woud	wood	would
7	tel	tell	tall
8	fell	fel	fall
9	sel	sal	sell
10	bel	bell	ball

Fill in the missing letter in the spelling words below.

th __ m   th __ se

m __ ke   som __

h __ r   woul __

t __ ll   fe __ l

s __ ll   bel __

Circle the words that rhyme in each row.

do	just	sell	bell
fell	she	tell	cool
drop	clear	mop	sub
had	fake	era	make

Lesson 21

TWO, HIM, MORE, TIME, HAS, LOOK, CUP, TRUCK, BUS, FUSS

Read the spelling words below and then write the words in the spaces provided.

two

him

more

time

has

look

cup

truck

bus

fuss

Complete the sentences using your spelling words.

We need _____ time.

The man drove the _____ .

The kids got on the school _____ .

The clock is used to tell _____ .

_____ at the bird in the sky.

Find and circle the spelling words in the puzzle.

BUS
CUP
FUSS
HAS
HIM
LOOK
MORE
TIME
TRUCK
TWO

C	T	I	M	E	V	F
U	M	T	Z	Q	K	U
P	O	E	R	O	B	S
S	R	C	O	U	C	S
H	E	L	M	H	C	O
J	A	I	T	W	O	K
N	H	S	D	B	U	S

21 Circle the correct spelling for each word.

1	tu	two	tou
2	hin	himm	him
3	more	mor	moar
4	time	tyme	tym
5	hass	haz	has
6	looc	luuk	look
7	cupp	kup	cup
8	truck	truk	truc
9	buss	bus	bass
10	fus	fuss	phus

Fill in the missing letter in the spelling words below.

t __ o   hi __

mo __ e   tim __

h __ s   lo __ k

c __ p   tr __ k

b __ s   fus __

Circle the words that rhyme in each row.

girls   fuss   am   bus

luck   truck   be   cup

look   hi   took   just

two   flu   do   right

Lesson 22

WRITE, GO, SEE, WAY, COULD, MY, LEG, LESS, MESS, PEG

Read the spelling words below and then write the words in the spaces provided.

write

go

see

way

could

my

leg

less

mess

peg

Complete the sentences using your spelling words.

I _____ with a pencil.

Glasses help me _____ better.

_____ favorite color is blue.

I broke my _____ .

This house is a dirty _____ .

Find and circle the spelling words in the puzzle.

COULD
GO
LEG
LESS
MESS
MY
PEG
SEE
WAY
WRITE

R	C	O	U	L	D	R
C	L	Y	U	E	Y	K
M	A	E	T	L	D	J
W	E	I	G	E	P	M
V	R	S	Q	S	E	M
W	C	Z	S	S	G	Y
V	R	G	O	S	E	E

22

Circle the correct spelling for each word.

1	rite	write	wright
2	go	goo	gao
3	cee	si	see
4	way	whey	wae
5	cood	coud	could
6	my	mi	miy
7	legg	lag	leg
8	les	lass	less
9	mes	mass	mess
10	peg	pegg	pag

Fill in the missing letter in the spelling words below.

wr __ te   g __

s __ e   w __ y

co __ ld   m __

l __ g   les __

m __ __ ss   p __ __g

Circle the words that rhyme in each row.

fun   leg   please   peg

mess   look   less   alien

take   bar   egg   make

mad   love   bye   my

Lesson 23

NUMBER, THAN, FIRST, WATER, BEEN, OIL, DRY, SKY, CRY, TRY

Read the spelling words below and then write the words in the spaces provided.

number

than

first

water

been

oil

dry

sky

cry

try

Complete the sentences using your spelling words.

My favorite _____ is ten.

The clouds are in the _____ .

When I am sad I _____ .

He won the race and got _____ place.

I like to drink _____ .

Find and circle the spelling words in the puzzle.

BEEN

CRY

DRY

FIRST

NUMBER

OIL

SKY

THAN

TRY

WATER

O	T	H	A	N	P	T
N	I	W	B	C	S	A
U	S	L	A	R	R	Y
M	K	J	I	T	R	Y
B	Y	F	S	T	E	T
E	B	B	E	E	N	R
R	D	C	D	R	Y	V

23

Circle the correct spelling for each word.

1	numba	numbr	number
2	than	thon	then
3	frst	first	phirst
4	wata	water	wotor
5	been	ben	byn
6	oal	iol	oil
7	dri	dryy	dry
8	ski	sky	scy
9	kry	cri	cry
10	tryy	try	tri

Fill in the missing letter in the spelling words below.

nu __ ber   th __ n

fir __ t   wa __ er

b __ en   o __ l

d __ y   sk __

c __ y   tr __

Circle the words that rhyme in each row.

try   tight   cry   throw

sky   moss   dry   catch

up   yup   out   pile

oil   see   high   coil

Lesson 24

PEOPLE, DAY, HID, FIND, LONG, DOWN, GAME, NAME, PLACE, SAME

Read the spelling words below and then write the words in the spaces provided.

people

day

hid

find

long

down

game

name

place

same

Complete the sentences using your spelling words.

My _____ is Sheila.

I can't _____ my shoes.

We both have the _____ hat.

There are lots of _____ at the beach today.

My favorite _____ is checkers.

Find and circle the spelling words in the puzzle.

DAY
DOWN
FIND
GAME
HID
LONG
NAME
PEOPLE
PLACE
SAME

U	P	D	U	E	L	D
G	I	E	M	C	O	O
H	A	A	O	Y	N	W
N	S	M	A	P	G	N
A	I	D	E	B	L	X
M	P	L	A	C	E	E
E	F	I	N	D	R	N

1	peaple	peeple	people
2	dayy	dai	day
3	hid	hidd	hiid
4	find	fin	phind
5	lonn	lawng	long
6	dwn	down	donn
7	game	gaym	gane
8	name	kname	nam
9	plac	place	plece
10	same	sime	saym

Fill in the missing letter in the spelling words below.

peo __ le   d __ y

h __ d   fi __ d

lo __ g   do __ n

ga __ e      na __ e

pl __ ce   s __ me

Circle the words that rhyme in each row.

game   name   fast   pace

top   place   lace   eager

bad   win   sad   lose

day   chuck   lay   turn

Lesson 25

TREE, COME, MADE, WAY, PART, PAY, SAY, STAY, TRAY, BAY

Read the spelling words below and then write the words in the spaces provided.

tree

come

made

way

part

pay

say

stay

tray

bay

Complete the sentences using your spelling words.

I built a _____ house.

I put food on the _____ .

My friend is going to _____ at my house.

_____ over here.

What did you _____ to me?

Find and circle the spelling words in the puzzle.

BAY
COME
MADE
PART
PAY
SAY
STAY
TRAY
TREE
WAY

S	M	Z	T	T	Y	T
T	P	A	R	R	Y	T
A	C	A	D	A	A	D
Y	P	C	S	E	L	Y
P	S	O	T	R	E	E
A	K	M	B	A	Y	B
Y	G	E	W	A	Y	U

1 tre   tree   trye

2 com   come   kome

3 made   mayd   maid

4 wai   woy   way

5 prt   port   part

6 pay   poy   pya

7 siy   say   see

8 stai   stoy   stay

9 trai   tray   tria

10 bai   bayy   bay

Fill in the missing letter in the spelling words below.

tr __ e   c __ me

m __ de   w __ y

p __ rt   pa __

sa __   st __ y

tr __ y   ba __

Circle the words that rhyme in each row.

bug   bay   how   tray

stay   found   say   old

don't   while   new   won't

part   feel   smart   job

Lesson 26

NICE, MICE, FIVE, DRIVE, HIVE, MINE, DIME, TIME, TWICE, DICE

Read the spelling words below and then write the words in the spaces provided.

nice

mice

five

drive

hive

mine

dime

time

twice

dice

Complete the sentences using your spelling words.

I rolled the _____.

What _____ is it?

A _____ is worth ten cents.

That pencil is _____ .

I love to _____ cars.

Find and circle the spelling words in the puzzle.

DICE
DIME
DRIVE
FIVE
HIVE
MICE
MINE
NICE
TIME
TWICE

H	I	V	E	F	N	L	D
D	I	C	E	E	I	I	I
D	G	X	N	M	C	R	M
M	R	I	W	E	E	A	E
I	M	I	C	T	I	M	E
C	X	I	V	A	N	Z	N
E	W	P	C	E	L	V	W
T	W	B	F	I	V	E	P

26 Circle the correct spelling for each word.

1 knice   nice   nic

2 mic   mice   micee

3 five   fiv   phive

4 driv   drive   druv

5 hive   hiv   hyv

6 myne   mene   mine

7 dime   dimy   dmei

8 tame   tim   time

9 twic   twyc   twice

10 dic   dice   dece

Fill in the missing letter in the spelling words below.

ni __ e   mi __ e

f __ ve   dr __ ve

h __ ve   mi __ e

d __ me   tim __

tw __ ce   di __ e

Circle the words that rhyme in each row.

go   dice   bang   twice

use   take   turn   muse

never   dime   says   time

why   cute   not   lie

Lesson 27

WEEK, SEEK, MEEK, SLEEP, DEEP, NEED, GREEN, FREE, HOUSE, SURE

Read the spelling words below and then write the words in the spaces provided.

week

seek

meek

sleep

deep

need

green

free

house

sure

Complete the sentences using your spelling words.

There are seven days in a _____.

Grass is _____.

Hide and _____ is fun.

I _____ in a bed.

I can't stand in the _____ end of the pool.

Find and circle the spelling words in the puzzle.

DEEP
FREE
GREEN
HOUSE
MEEK
NEED
SEEK
SLEEP
SURE
WEEK

D	E	E	P	P	I	D	H
Z	C	F	E	S	U	R	E
U	C	E	F	R	E	E	N
W	L	G	R	E	E	N	H
S	E	N	I	D	F	S	O
K	Q	E	E	R	Z	E	U
B	Q	K	K	E	W	E	S
M	E	E	K	A	D	K	E

27 Circle the correct spelling for each word.

1	weak	weec	week
2	seak	seek	seec
3	meek	meak	miek
4	sleep	sleap	selep
5	deup	deap	deep
6	nead	neede	need
7	green	grne	greene
8	fri	free	friye
9	huose	hous	house
10	shur	sher	sure

Fill in the missing letter in the spelling words below.

we __ k   se __ k

me __ k   sl __ ep

d __ ep   nee __

gr __ en   fre __

ho __ se   __ ure

Circle the words that rhyme in each row.

week	leak	ever	so	
yes	able	booth	tooth
one	call	done	work
better	never	ever	best

Read the spelling words below and then write the words in the spaces provided.

hello

bye

summer

moon

spoon

roof

tooth

smooth

pool

noon

Complete the sentences using your spelling words.

It is hot during the _____.

I eat soup with a _____.

The dentist fixed my _____ .

I went swimming in the _____ .

The chimney is on the _____ .

Find and circle the spelling words in the puzzle.

BYE
HELLO
MOON
NOON
POOL
ROOF
SMOOTH
SPOON
SUMMER
TOOTH

S	T	R	L	X	H	K	I
F	U	O	O	T	H	H	W
M	O	M	O	O	T	E	T
P	O	O	M	C	F	L	O
U	M	O	X	E	I	L	O
S	F	W	N	X	R	O	T
W	S	P	O	O	N	G	H
B	Y	E	N	O	O	N	K

28

Circle the correct spelling for each word.

1   helo   hello   hilow

2   bi   bye   bie

3   summer   summr   sumer

4   moon   muun   maon

5   spoun   spoan   spoon

6   ruof   rooph   roof

7   toot   tuth   tooth

8   smoov   smoth   smooth

9   pool   puul   poul

10 nuun   noon   noun

Fill in the missing letter in the spelling words below.

he __ lo   by __

sum __ er   moo __

sp __ on   roo __

to __ th   smoo __ h

po __ l   __ oon

Circle the words that rhyme in each row.

pool   what   stool   lot

moon   spoon   bar   logic

bar   why   don't   car

also   oh   cool   mule

Lesson 29

WINTER, COLD, NOSE, HOSE, HOLE, ROLE, ROSE, SPOKE, WOKE, SMOKE

Read the spelling words below and then write the words in the spaces provided.

winter

cold

nose

hose

hole

role

rose

spoke

woke

smoke

Complete the sentences using your spelling words.

It is cold during _____.

The freezer is _____.

A _____ is a red flower.

_____ came from the chimney.

I blew my _____ into a tissue.

Find and circle the spelling words in the puzzle.

COLD
HOLE
HOSE
NOSE
ROLE
ROSE
SMOKE
SPOKE
WINTER
WOKE

F	S	P	O	K	E	R	E
H	O	S	E	F	G	L	P
R	S	O	S	E	O	R	C
O	T	M	L	H	E	W	O
S	N	O	O	T	F	O	L
E	R	O	N	K	D	K	D
M	D	I	S	G	E	E	Y
D	W	H	O	E	E	V	J

29

Circle the correct spelling for each word.

1	wintr	winter	whinter
2	cold	could	cole
3	nose	knose	nos
4	hosa	hose	hase
5	hole	hol	whole
6	role	rol	wrole
7	rase	rose	wrose
8	spoke	spok	spocke
9	wok	whoke	woke
10	smok	smoke	smake

Fill in the missing letter in the spelling words below.

wi __ ter   co__d

no __ e   ho__e

h __ le   ro __ e

r __ se   sp __ ke

wo__ e   smo__e

Circle the words that rhyme in each row.

smoke   glide   like   woke

about   cool   hose   rose

rob   greek   nice   mob

nest   curl   bird   hurl

Lesson 30

FALL, WIND, RAIN, SNOW, GROW, LOW, SHOW, BELOW, FLOW, CLOUD

Read the spelling words below and then write the words in the spaces provided.

fall

wind

rain

snow

grow

low

show

below

flow

cloud

Complete the sentences using your spelling words.

The _____ is in the sky.

Rain helps the flower _____ .

The leaves change during ____ .

_____ helps the grass grow.

The _____ melted when it got warmer.

Find and circle the spelling words in the puzzle.

BELOW
CLOUD
FALL
FLOW
GROW
LOW
RAIN
SHOW
SNOW
WIND

C	L	S	N	O	W	R
W	L	O	G	I	H	A
F	W	O	W	R	W	I
L	I	F	U	O	O	N
O	N	U	L	D	V	W
W	D	E	S	H	O	W
O	B	F	A	L	L	Y

30 — Circle the correct spelling for each word.

1 fal   faul   fall

2 win   wind   whind

3 rain   rian   wrain

4 snow   sown   snkow

5 grwo   grow   gwro

6 low   loww   laow

7 shaw   show   shou

8 below   bilow   belou

9 flou   flow   fluow

10 clowd   kloud   cloud

Fill in the missing letter in the spelling words below.

f __ ll   __ ind

ra __ n   sn __ w

g __ ow   lo __

sh __ w   be __ ow

fl __ w   c __ oud

Circle the words that rhyme in each row.

fall   below   stall   flow

block   snow   friend   low

lunch   shut   rain   train

cloud   news   loud   never

Lesson 31

BOTH, MUCH, LUNCH, MATH,
LOOK, TOOK, MOOD, WOOD,
FOOT, FOOD

Read the spelling words below and then write the words in the spaces provided.

both

much

lunch

math

look

took

mood

wood

foot

food

Complete the sentences using your spelling words.

_____ is the second meal of the day.

The lumberjack chops _____.

I eat _____ when I'm hungry.

I put a _____ on my foot.

I am in a good _____ today.

Find and circle the spelling words in the puzzle.

BOTH
FOOD
FOOT
LOOK
LUNCH
MATH
MOOD
MUCH
TOOK
WOOD

M	L	U	N	C	H	P
F	U	B	O	T	H	K
O	I	C	K	F	O	A
O	M	O	H	O	F	W
T	O	A	T	Y	O	O
L	T	F	T	B	O	O
M	O	O	D	H	D	D

1   both   boht   bath

2   muhc   much   mach

3   lunck   lunch   lanch

4   math   maht   moth

5   look   loak   looc

6   touk   tuuk   took

7   moad   muud   mood

8   woud   wood   woodd

9   fout   foet   foot

10 food   foud   fuud

Fill in the missing letter in the spelling words below.

bo__h   muc __

l__nch   ma __h

l __ ok   to __k

moo__   woo __

fo__ t   foo __

Circle the words that rhyme in each row.

salad   wood   cup   stood

birth   go   look   took

foot   food   up   soot

great   math   mast   path

WHY, FOUR, FIVE, AIR, ALSO, COW, TOWN, PLOW, DOWN, BROWN

Read the spelling words below and then write the words in the spaces provided.

why

four

five

air

also

cow

town

plow

down

brown

Complete the sentences using your spelling words.

The plane flies in the _____.

Dirt is the color _____.

_____ plus four equals nine.

_____ plus five equals nine.

_____ did you do that?

Find and circle the spelling words in the puzzle.

AIR
ALSO
BROWN
COW
DOWN
FIVE
FOUR
PLOW
TOWN
WHY

E	L	D	O	W	N	E
F	C	O	W	A	I	R
I	O	B	R	O	W	N
P	A	U	W	N	N	F
L	L	E	R	W	Y	I
O	S	U	O	H	Z	V
W	O	T	W	Y	G	E

Circle the correct spelling for each word.

1 whyy   whi   why

2 for   four   fore

3 five   fave   fuva

4 ari   oair   air

5 also   aols   olso

6 ocow   kow   cow

7 toun   town   touen

8 plow   plough   plou

9 dwn   dawn   down

10 brne   brawn   brown

Fill in the missing letter in the spelling words below.

w__y   fo__r

f__ve   a__r

a__so   co__

to__n   pl__w

d__wn   brow__

Circle the words that rhyme in each row.

me   twin   down   brown

for   far   more   so

why   what   try   win

cow   hat   zoom   wow

Lesson 33

Read the spelling words below and then write the words in the spaces provided.

soap

coat

boat

float

trip

loan

help

here

home

toast

Complete the sentences using your spelling words.

I wash my hands with _____.

The class went on a field _____.

_____ me solve this problem.

I ate _____ for breakfast.

The _____ is at the dock.

Find and circle the spelling words in the puzzle.

BOAT
COAT
FLOAT
HELP
HERE
HOME
LOAN
SOAP
TOAST
TRIP

X	H	O	C	O	A	T	C
S	L	O	I	H	E	L	P
U	O	B	M	T	F	B	L
D	P	A	S	E	L	O	O
J	P	A	P	E	O	A	A
G	O	T	R	I	A	T	N
T	T	E	G	Q	T	Q	H
Q	H	T	R	I	P	Y	R

33 Circle the correct spelling for each word.

1	saop	soop	soap
2	coat	coaut	cote
3	boot	baout	boat
4	flate	flowt	float
5	trip	tryp	trap
6	laon	loan	luan
7	help	halp	hulp
8	here	hure	heyr
9	homy	home	hum
10	toust	taost	toast

Fill in the missing letter in the spelling words below.

s __ ap   co __ t

bo__ t   __loat

tr __ p   loa __

h __ lp   her __

ho__ e   toas __

Circle the words that rhyme in each row.

toast   sit   roast   so

coat   you   did   wrote

hand   float   boat   not

it   hand   trip   lip

Lesson 34

DOES, END, BEND, SEND, LEND, BOY, GIRL, ONLY, MOVE, OFF

Read the spelling words below and then write the words in the spaces provided.

does

end

bend

send

lend

boy

girl

only

move

off

Complete the sentences using your spelling words.

I _____ a letter.

The _____ is named Bill.

The _____ is named Lucy.

Turn the lights _____ .

Can you _____ me a hand?

Find and circle the spelling words in the puzzle.

BEND
BOY
DOES
END
GIRL
LEND
MOVE
OFF
ONLY
SEND

O	F	F	L	E	N	D
E	D	H	M	L	L	L
E	O	O	J	O	R	R
N	E	N	B	I	V	D
D	S	L	G	E	N	E
K	H	Y	B	E	N	F
B	O	Y	S	W	O	D

Circle the correct spelling for each word.

1 does   deos   duss

2 endd   ende   end

3 bennd   bend   bund

4 send   sand   sendd

5 lend   land   lund

6 boi   boye   boy

7 gril   gyurl   girl

8 onli   only   onlye

9 move   mave   moov

10 ofe   aff   off

Fill in the missing letter in the spelling words below.

d __ es   en __

be __ d   sen __

le __ d   bo __

g __ rl   onl __

m __ ve   __ ff

Circle the words that rhyme in each row.

hat   move   groove   right

end   live   die   bend

send   bet   bend   found

girl   gone   curl   cry

Lesson 35

PAGE, AGE, CAGE, WAGE, SOIL, TOIL, VERY, STILL, MILL, GREAT

Read the spelling words below and then write the words in the spaces provided.

page

age

cage

wage

soil

toil

very

still

mill

great

Complete the sentences using your spelling words.

The worker gets paid a _____ .

I planted seeds in the _____ .

I turned the _____ .

The dog is in the _____ .

I feel _____ .

Find and circle the spelling words in the puzzle.

AGE
CAGE
GREAT
MILL
PAGE
SOIL
STILL
TOIL
VERY
WAGE

M	W	D	A	L	C	Y
I	Z	A	I	G	R	G
L	S	O	G	E	E	R
L	S	B	V	E	T	E
S	T	I	L	L	O	A
I	P	A	G	E	I	T
C	A	G	E	X	L	X

1 payg   puge   page

2 age   ayg   aga

3 cayg   cuge   cage

4 wage   wayg   woge

5 soul   soil   sail

6 tail   toil   tule

7 very   vury   vary

8 stil   stull   still

9 mil   mill   mull

10 grite   grayt   great

Fill in the missing letter in the spelling words below.

pa __ e   ag __

c __ ge   wag __

so __ l   toi __

ve __ y   stil __

m __ ll   grea __

Circle the words that rhyme in each row.

wage   age   why   are

quit   soil   take   toil

still   sat   mill   move

may   great   lash   mate

Lesson 36

QUIT, QUEEN, QUILT, QUACK, DUCK, BIRD, BAT, AWAY, EVEN, ODD

Read the spelling words below and then write the words in the spaces provided.

quit

queen

quilt

quack

duck

bird

bat

away

even

odd

Complete the sentences using your spelling words.

The _____ flew away .

The _____ quacked.

The _____ comes out at night.

Two is an _____ number.

The bird flew _____ .

Find and circle the spelling words in the puzzle.

AWAY
BAT
BIRD
DUCK
EVEN
ODD
QUACK
QUEEN
QUILT
QUIT

B	A	E	V	E	N	N
Q	A	W	U	O	E	P
I	U	T	A	E	W	K
Q	B	I	U	Y	C	O
U	I	Q	L	U	J	D
I	R	G	D	T	V	D
T	D	Q	U	A	C	K

1	quit	quat	quite
2	quwen	queen	kween
3	quiltt	quilye	quilt
4	kwack	qwock	quack
5	dack	ducc	duck
6	burd	bird	byrd
7	bat	bot	batt
8	away	oway	aweay
9	aven	evan	even
10	od	odd	ad

Fill in the missing letter in the spelling words below.

qu __ t   quee __

qu __ l t   qua __ k

d __ ck   bi __ d

__ at   aw __ y

ev __ n   od __

Circle the words that rhyme in each row.

odd   nope   nod   yes

bat   mat   pay   off

quack   sand   lack   land

duck   queen   mean   met

Made in the USA
Las Vegas, NV
04 April 2024

88246030R00083